New Mexico

BY M. J. YORK

The Child's World

Published by The Child's World®
1980 Lookout Drive • Mankato, MN 56003-1705
800-599-READ • www.childsworld.com

ACKNOWLEDGMENTS
The Child's World®: Mary Berendes, Publishing Director
The Design Lab: Design and production
Red Line Editorial: Editorial direction

PHOTO CREDITS: Peter Mautsch/Bigstock, cover, 1, 3; Matt Kania/Map
Hero, Inc., 4, 5; Greg Panosian/iStockphoto, 7; Mary J. Lewis/iStockphoto, 9;
iStockphoto, 10; Shutterstock Images, 11; Melanie Dabovich/AP Images, 13,
Greg Panosian/iStockphoto, 15; Bill Moffitt/AP Images, 17; AP Images, 19;
David Parsons/iStockphoto, 21; One Mile Up, 22; Quarter-dollar coin image
from the United States Mint, 22

LIBRARY OF CONGRESS CATALOGING-IN-PUBLICATION DATA
York, M. J., 1983–
  New Mexico / by M.J. York.
      p. cm.
Includes bibliographical references and index.
ISBN 978-1-60253-475-9 (library bound : alk. paper)
1. New Mexico—Juvenile literature. I. Title.

F796.3.Y67 2010
978.9—dc22

                                        2010019193

Printed in the United States of America in Mankato, Minnesota.
July 2010
F11538

On the cover:
El San Miguel
Mission is in
Santa Fe,
New Mexico.

CONTENTS

Geography

Let's explore New Mexico! New Mexico is in the southwestern United States. Mexico is to the south.

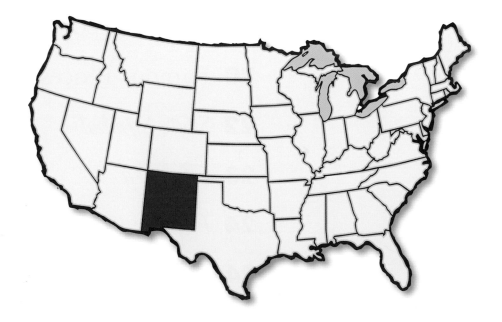

UTAH

COLORADO

OKLAHOMA

ARIZONA

Taos •

Los Alamos •

★ **Santa Fe**

• Gallup

Rio Rancho •

Albuquerque •

Santa Rosa •

NEW MEXICO

• Fort Sumner

Rio Grande

Socorro •

Roswell •

• Alamogordo

• Silver City

Carlsbad •

• Las Cruces

Carlsbad Caverns
National Park

NORTH

WEST   EAST

SOUTH

TEXAS

MEXICO

Cities

Santa Fe is the capital of New Mexico. Albuquerque is the largest city in the state. Both cities are very old. Santa Fe was founded in the early 1600s. Albuquerque was founded in 1706. Las Cruces is another well-known city.

New Mexico is known as "the Land of Enchantment."

Santa Fe is known for its history and old **adobe** houses. ▶

Land

New Mexico is one of the driest states in the United States. It has deserts, mountains, and dry **plains**. The Rio Grande is the longest river in the state.

The Rio Grande cuts through the center of New Mexico. ▶

Plants and Animals

New Mexico's state flower is the yucca. It is a desert plant with a white flower. The state tree is the piñon. Pine nuts come from this tree. The state bird is the roadrunner. It lives in the desert.

The yucca can live in areas that have little water. ▶

People and Work

Almost 2 million people live in New Mexico. Many people in the state work in **science** and **technology**. Mining and **manufacturing** are large **industries**. Chili peppers are grown in New Mexico. Many artists work here, too.

A man sells chili peppers in Albuquerque, New Mexico. ▶

13

History

Long before people from Europe came to the area, Native Americans built houses from adobe. In the 1500s, people from Spain explored the area. They built cities in the 1600s. In 1848, the United States took control of the area. New Mexico became the forty-seventh state on January 6, 1912.

Some Native American artifacts found in New Mexico are thousands of years old.

Taos is a New Mexico city thought to be 1,000 years old. ▶

Ways of Life

Mexican **culture** and the Spanish language are important in New Mexico. Almost one-third of families in New Mexico speak Spanish at home. Native American culture is important in the state, too. The state is home to three large Native American groups: the Pueblo, the Navajo, and the Apache.

People come to a yearly event in Albuquerque to see hundreds of hot air balloons soar through the sky.

Dancers wear colorful costumes and celebrate culture in Roswell, New Mexico. ▶

Famous People

Some well-known people of the West came to New Mexico. Outlaw Billy the Kid ran from the law in this state. Mountain man Kit Carson lived here. Singer John Denver was born in New Mexico. Painter Georgia O'Keeffe created beautiful art in the state.

Georgia O'Keeffe was born in Wisconsin and spent time in New Mexico later in her life. ▶

Famous Places

The Carlsbad Caverns are a group of huge caves in New Mexico. Visitors can walk through them. Some people in the town of Roswell believe they have seen **UFOs**. The town has a gathering every year for people to discuss aliens.

Some parts of the Carlsbad Caverns are yet to be explored. ▶

State Symbols

Seal

The state seal of New Mexico has two eagles. One eagle stands for the United States. It is protecting the other eagle, which stands for Mexico. Go to childsworld.com/links for a link to New Mexico's state Web site, where you can get a firsthand look at the state seal.

Flag

The state flag of New Mexico is yellow with a red **design** in the middle. The Native American design stands for the sun.

Quarter

New Mexico's state quarter has an outline of the state and a sun symbol. The quarter came out in 2008.

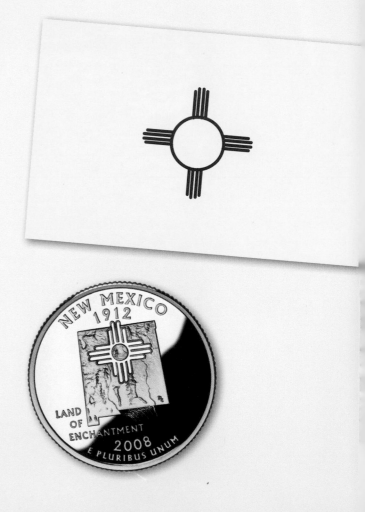

Glossary

adobe (uh-DOH-bee): Adobe is a type of brick made from mud and straw. Native Americans in New Mexico built houses from adobe.

artifacts (ART-uh-facts): Artifacts are objects made by people. Scientists have found artifacts in New Mexico left by people from long ago.

culture (KUL-chur): Culture refers to the art and manners of a group of people. Mexican and Native American culture are important in New Mexico.

design (dih-ZYNE): A design is a drawing or a shape. New Mexico's state flag has a sun design in the center.

enchantment (en-CHANT-munt): Enchantment is charm or delight. New Mexico is called "the Land of Enchantment."

industries (IN-duh-streez): Industries are businesses, companies, or areas of trade. Mining and manufacturing are important industries in New Mexico.

manufacturing (man-yuh-FAK-chur-ing): Manufacturing is the task of making items with machines. Many people work in manufacturing in New Mexico.

plains (PLAYNZ): Plains are areas of flat land that do not have many trees. New Mexico has dry plains.

science (SYE-unss): Science is the study of the world and nature. Some people in New Mexico have jobs in science.

seal (SEEL): A seal is a symbol a state uses for government business. New Mexico's seal has eagles to stand for the United States and Mexico.

symbols (SIM-bulz): Symbols are pictures or things that stand for something else. Symbols appear on New Mexico's seal.

technology (tek-NAWL-uh-jee): Technology is scientific knowledge applied to practical things. The technology industry is important in New Mexico.

UFOs (YOU-EFF-OHZ): UFOs is short for *unidentified flying objects*, or alien spaceships. Some people in New Mexico believe they have seen UFOs.

Further Information

Books

James, Helen Foster. *E is for Enchantment: A New Mexico Alphabet*. Chelsea, MI: Sleeping Bear Press, 2004.

Keller, Laurie. *The Scrambled States of America*. New York: Henry Holt, 2002.

Walker, Cynthia. *New Mexico*. New York: Children's Press, 2004.

Web Sites

Visit our Web site for links about New Mexico: *childsworld.com/links*

Note to Parents, Teachers, and Librarians: We routinely verify our Web links to make sure they are safe and active sites. So encourage your readers to check them out!

Index